Off The Grid Survival

Beginners Grid Down Survival Tips, Tricks and Long Term Survival Strategies for Preppers

Steve Rayder

SOUTHSHORE
PUBLICATIONS & DISTRIBUTION

www.southshorepublications.com

© 2015 by SouthShore Publications & Distribution.

ISBN-13: 978-1514876749

ISBN-10: 1514876744

CONTENTS

INTRODUCTION 7

    The Importance of Being Prepared.................................7

    How to Prepare 9

BUGGING OUT OR BUGGING IN? 11

    Bugging In 11

    Bugging Out 13

    Be Flexible..16

OFF THE GRID FARMING 17

    Compost 17

    Watering Crops 18

    Drilling a Homemade Well..18

    Pest Prevention 19

    Fencing 20

    Raised Beds 20

    Pesticides 20

    Home Remedies...20

    Maintaining your Crops Year After Year 21

ANIMAL FARMING 23

    What Animals To Get..23

    Educate Yourself 23

    Feeding Your Livestock..24

    Prepare for the Worst 25

STORAGE AND PRESERVATION 26

    Water Bath Canning...26

HIGH PRESSURE CANNING 27

PRESERVING MEAT 28

SMOKING AND JERKY 28

SALTING AND CURING 29

HOW TO PRESERVE EGGS FOR MONTHS 29

RENEWABLE ENERGY **31**

SOLAR POWER 31

MINI SOLAR PANELS 32

WIND POWER 32

HOME SECURITY **34**

BASIC FIRST AID 34

MEDICAL SUPPLIES 35

COMMUNICATION PLANS AND RENDEZVOUS POINTS 36

HAND TO HAND COMBAT TRAINING (SELF DEFENSE) 36

WEAPONS TRAINING 37

RETREATING 38

SUCCESS IN THE OFF GRID WORLD **39**

COMMUNITY 39

PREPARATION 39

PRACTICE 41

MONEY 42

LOCATION 43

THANKS FOR READING! **44**

Introduction

Are you concerned about the possibility of a disaster meaning that the grid will go down? Do you want to learn more about how to survive off the grid in a disaster situation and how to prepare for such an event ahead of time? Then this is the perfect book for you.

The Importance of Being Prepared

Off grid living has growing in popularity in recent years, with more and more survivalists and preppers becoming interested in it, but what is it?

Living off grid means being totally self-sustaining and not relying on an electricity being delivered to you by an extremely vulnerable, and hard to repair, grid. It also means not relying on a grocery store for food and water. It can also mean foregoing traditional healthcare and visits to the doctor.

Simply put, it's like pioneer living in the modern world. You've carved out your own little slice of heaven on earth and wish to live in a self-reliant way with your family.

There are several reasons to choose off grid living, perhaps you are tired of world governments tracking your every move. Maybe you're tired of the noisy life of city and suburban living. Maybe you are ready to get back to your roots or you have a strong desire to test yourself to the limits in order to see what you are capable of. Perhaps you don't want to live off grid, but you may be preparing to do so in case of some global calamity.

Whatever your reasons for going off the grid, be prepared for a different set of challenges, because a pioneering life is a hard life. The purpose of this book is to help you think about the important things that off grid living entails and how to deal with them. There will be things that you will need to have planned out and prepared in advance in order to enhance the likelihood of your success.

If you really want to get ready for an extreme case of off the grid living, you will need to prepare now and essentially live as if emergency services aren't just a phone call away, neither is a hospital and neither is a grocery store.

In the world today mankind shares a relatively unique set of challenges. These challenges arise from our own ingenuity; we have created so much technology that we have become quite dependent upon it. In essence, we've lost our roots in agriculture and relative self-sufficiency.

The challenge in this overly connected world of reliance is one of simple survival. If a catastrophic event were to cause the power to go out, and multitudes of people to perish, what will happen to the everyday average Joe?

Let's let that sink in; the power's gone out, the majority of farmers (livestock and plant alike) are no longer alive or able to continue their farming operations. The grocery store is running dangerously low on consumables and there's no end in sight. It's pretty heavy stuff to think about but if you have a family or others who depend on you, it's very likely something that weighs heavily on your mind from time to time if you're not properly prepared.

For ease of remembrance let's call this hypothetical situation SHTF (s*** hits the fan). This situation is terrifying enough from the pure loss of life alone, but will grow ever more frightening as the situation darkens.

People have become accustomed to the life we live. We are used to the idea of being able to pick up the components of lunch and dinner at a store down the road from us. It allows us to not think too far ahead, do less work on the dinner routine and more time doing something we really enjoy.

Something that impacts the comfort zone that we are so used to, can lead to a disastrous chain reaction. After Hurricane Katrina hit New Orleans it took just 3 days before there were roving bands of looters pillaging stores for food, water and supplies to survive.

How to Prepare

So what does one do to prepare themselves? How do you ensure that your family will survive a scenario such as this and stay surviving for the long term?

Recent years have seen a huge rise in the popularity of prepping. Prepping of course is most notable to many people as those "crazy" people on the discovery channel who spend their whole income on preparing for some whacko event that may or may not ever come, forsaking comfortable living now for a more stable future.

While the fundamentals of it are correct, not every prepper believes in some over the top scenario involving aliens, angels, large government conspiracies or zombies leading to catastrophic breakdown of society. Neither does every prepper spend every cent they've earned preparing for such a scenario. A good prepper typically takes a practical approach to surviving the short term, while spending more time looking for a feasible long term solution. So where does one start? How do you know what to do exactly? Firstly, you need to choose a location…

Bugging out or Bugging in?

So the SHTF and now you've got a choice to make. Do you stay at home, comfortable that the amount of supplies you've built up, and the sustainable living plan you have put into place will sustain you and your family until either the scenario is fixed or the supplies run out? Or do you try and find greener pastures to set up your new off the grid lifestyle?

Bugging In

If staying put is your choice for you then you've selected bugging in. Meaning you don't get up and go as soon as the bad news hits. Rather you are ready to wait it out somewhat comfortably in your home until the bad is fixed or it's time to move out and try to scavenge. Typically this option should be reserved for suburban and rural dwellers as the sheer population density in larger urban areas is more likely to result in looting, murder, theft and ransom.

Also, you're going to need some space to collect water (something that you can't do in an apartment), to grow your crops and to keep any livestock you may be rearing. When bugging in, food and water will be your main concerns.

The food problem is easy to understand and is the first thing that usually comes to mind. Gardening and growing your own crops is a great way to ensure there's something on the table for supper, but what if you have bad crops?

If you've planned to bug in, then you've likely planned for the hardships that come along with self-sufficiency. A great idea is to can and store food. This is something that you should learn ahead of time and will be an invaluable skill to have when times get tough.

Gardening now and using what you need while saving the rest will help you better understand exactly what you will need to produce should the grocery store be unavailable. Imagine a scenario where the lights are off for over a year and the first winter lasts longer than normal. Your garden is planted late and then a freak freeze moves through and decimates more than half of what you've planted. Scary situation, right? Well if you've been methodically preparing, it's only as scary as running to the cellar and grabbing a few cans of vegetables.

Now if you've been preparing for an emergency scenario there's a good likelihood that you've got some water stored, but if this could turn into a long term situation, how do you replenish your stores of water? Water purification can be a bit mystifying to many people, after all we've lived with plumbing so long that we have forgotten or never knew ways of collecting safe drinking water. The most important rule is boiling for sanitation. Boiling water is the best way to kill off any dangerous organisms in the water. So hopefully you've a reliable, sustainable way of boiling water. If not, there are other ways of doing things.

Making a fire every time you need to boil some water in a SHTF scenario is not the best idea for a few reasons. Not only will it use precious fuel (remember everyone who has survived will be cutting down fire wood) but it will also draw attention to you in the form of smoke.

So my number one recommendation for any prepper is to invest in a Berkey water filter. These things can turn any water into fresh, safe drinking water with no power at all. I really do mean any water, they can handle swimming pool water, river water and pretty much anything else you can throw at it. They work by simply using gravity to draw the water through the filter. So no need for fires and no need for power. Prefect for SHTF/off the grid living.

Bugging Out

Bugging out is for those situations which require you to evacuate the area. Say a natural disaster has made the area you live uninhabitable, or a chemical agent has been introduced which means, it's not only hazardous to your health to stay there, but food and game from the area are no longer a viable option for you.

Bugging out means getting out quickly. Being able to get out quickly means having the framework of your imminent escape already well thought out and prepared.

Many people are familiar with BOB or bug out bag. BOB is the go to bag that is packed and ready to get you on the road to safety, all you need to do is grab it and go. In many cases, a bug out bag may not be enough. Some people consider a get home bag as well. This stays in your car and is what you need to make it home should catastrophe strike while you are away from home. I have a book dedicated to bug out bags and the items you should keep in them that you can find by searching my name on Amazon if you would like to really get a great bug out bag ready to go.

Bugging out doesn't mean you don't need to be prepared for the same scenarios as bugging in. You will need to find sources of nourishment and water. But you will also have to make or find sources of shelter and heat too making things a lot harder. The main difference is that you are on the go while doing this, which makes everything you do a lot more challenging.

Bugging out requires immense preparation as foraging and hunting skills don't just appear overnight. Preparing to bug out includes thinking about a variety of scenarios and how to handle them. The biggest two challenges will be food and water.

Firstly let's talk about food. Most people will have some food supplies that they will plan on taking with them when bugging out, or they may have some supplies already at a designated bug out area, but this won't last forever. You can always forage but unless you're highly experienced, it can be very hard to sustain yourself in this way, even when there aren't thousands of other people with the same idea as you foraging all the wild food for themselves. You could always supplement your diet by going out hunting but similarly, a lot of wild animals will be hunted to the brink of extinction within months due to the size of the human population and how much it outweighs wildlife.

In some areas that are less populated, hunting may well be a viable option for a time however. In order to be well prepared for hunting you must first understand what it is you need. Thanks to sporting goods stores and merchandising contracts many people today believe they have to have the latest and greatest in hunting technology from brands A or B, or the best thermal imaging scope, or a rangefinder, or a red dot on their crossbow or rifle. However, your grandfather didn't have access to scent block technology and he probably did just fine on his yearly hunting trip. Knowledge and experience is the key, not a high tech weapon.

Successful hunting requires patience, you must be willing to sit silently in one or two spots for the better part of the day. You must be willing to endure some rain, or snow, or cold or heat. Depending on your surroundings after a catastrophe, you need to choose whether you would prefer to hunt with a rifle/shotgun or a bow. The size of your game will also be a huge consideration. Get some advice from the store owner where you are buying your gear so that you know the weapon you have will be suitable for what you are intending to hunt.

So you know what you're going to hunt with. Do you know how to use the weapon you've selected? Do you know how to be precise with it? Since you are a prepper, you had better be practicing so you can be good at it. If not then get some practice with your weapon.

Bugging out raises the same concerns with regards to water. As with bugging in, the smoke from the fire that you use to boil your water will give away your location and potentially attract danger. You can buy a smaller size Berkey however that will serve you well or you can use Iodine, Bleach or even water purification tablets.

To purify water with bleach you need remove as much sediment from the water as possible, then add 4 drops of bleach per liter of warm water and leave it to sit for half an hour. If you can't warm your water in any way then just double the dose but it will taste quite bleachy. Iodine can also be used in the same way and it's safer for human consumption than bleach, although bleach is fine when diluted and not consumed for extended periods of time.

Be Flexible

Of course these suggestions would not be complete without reminding of the most important factors, planning and flexibility.

While you can resolve to bug out or resolve to bug in, not every scenario you encounter will actually allow for this. In essence, if you're preparing to stay put, you should still be prepared to get moving and vice versa.

Off the Grid Farming

Farming in the off grid world requires going back to the old ways of doing things. To provide well rounded nutrition for yourself and your dependents, several variables must be considered.

Fruits and Vegetables are completely dependent on the soil, so you need to look after that soil. You need to estimate how much food you'll need and assume that you will lose some to bugs, pests, pestilence and weather.

Compost

Perhaps one of the greatest ways to ensure fertile land and great crops is by utilizing composting. Composting means you take any and all bio-degradable trash and place it in a bin or contained area. Mix into this animal excrement, grass clippings, pulled weeds and then stir the whole mixture randomly throughout the year for a great compost.

As time goes on the contents of your compost will begin the natural breakdown process. Eventually this will all become very fertile compost to be used as a planting soil or topsoil. You will simply mix in the broken down contents from the compost pile into the soil where you are intending to grow crops and then plant away.

Composting is an all-around great natural fertilizer and will help you safely dispose of some common forms of garbage in a non-wasteful way. Every few months the compost pile should be tumbled, stirred or turned to facilitate bacterial movement and breakdown of the contents. It's pretty simple really!

Watering Crops

Irrigation or watering will be terribly important to thriving plant life. If the power is off and there's no more water company, how do you ensure water not only for you and your family; but also for your precious crops?

The answer is relatively simple actually. You just have to utilize groundwater. Try drilling or driving your own well and tapping into one of the most underrated resources available, water. In most areas you can generally find water after drilling or driving 20 feet down below the surface.

Drilling a Homemade Well

To get to our ground water, a great option is to get a hand pump and to drill your own well.

Before undertaking any project like this, you need to choose the right spot. Stay at least 50 feet or more away from a known sewer line or septic tank, not only can this contaminate the water, but also any other well service on that same groundwater line.

The depth of the well will depend on the water table in your area. The water table is the level below the ground where the soil becomes saturated with water. Information on the water table in your local area can be found online. If it's over 20 feet below the surface then you will probably need to get a professional to help you out.

Now this isn't a guide to digging a well and installing a pump but to give you an idea here's an overview:

If you're going to do it yourself, then step one is digging a hole. The difficulty of this task is going to vary wildly based on the type of ground you're digging into. The simplest way to do this is by using a Post Hole Auger and a couple of handle extensions so that you can drill down as far as you can

Then you're going to want to insert some PVC pipe into the hole to be used as the casing. Next you will need something like a sand point connected to a length of metal pipe, which you will then drive even further down until you hit water. You will know when you hot water because you can hear it in the pipe as you're driving it down. Then you simply connect up the hand pump, prime it and you're ready to go.

I probably made that sound a lot easier than it is, there is a lot of work involved. Luckily for us, a very helpful chap on YouTube has put together a playlist of himself carrying out this exact process. So you can take a look and judge for yourself:

https://www.youtube.com/playlist?list=PLSw6mhcLSL-MSuEdBAg9p9I2rUCqhGctd

Pest Prevention

One huge issue with farming is always going to be pests. These can be in the form of garden bugs that eat crops and spread pestilence or in the form of the pesky rabbit for example. If you have livestock you may even have problems with foxes trying to eat your chickens. So how do you protect your precious food?

Fencing

You can always run fencing around your garden, the size of the animals you are dealing with will determine the size of fence you need. This is definitely something you will want to set up in advance as fencing materials such as wire mesh will be very hard to come by in a SHTF scenario.

Raised Beds

Another great way to prevent some of the smaller vermin from destroying your plants is to plant in raised beds. Raising a bed 3 or more feet off the ground can help to deter rabbits, moles and other animals of their ilk from wreaking havoc on your food plots.

Pesticides

You can treat with pesticides, there are both natural and unnatural versions available, natural are considered to be healthier for the eco system and humans, unnatural are more likely to destroy or eradicate the issue. Also, in a SHTF situation, you can't just go an buy some pesticide so this might not be the best option.

Home Remedies

There are all sorts of home remedies that could be tried as well. Deer have impeccable sense of smell, putting small clumps of human hair around your crops is said to keep them away. Many animals are frightened by startling noises, putting aluminum pie tins tied to strings that will clatter can help to keep some pests away as well.

Maintaining your Crops Year After Year

It's important to keep in mind how fragile soil can really be. If you wish to have successful harvests year after year, you must take care of your soil. The same crops should not be planted in the same spot every year. This will contribute to erosion of the soil and a loss of nutrients.

A second factor is pesticide resistance. In essence, the more pesticide used to prevent a certain threat to your crops, the more likely that pest will build up a tolerance to what's used. This will create a cyclical effect in which more and more pesticides will need to be used each year. To break up pests and preserve your crops consider some of the following options:

- Disperse crops throughout your garden. Pests are generally specific to a certain plant, making it easier for them to feast when all your tomatoes, for example, are in the same spot in the garden.
- Water early or use drip or root irrigation systems. Wet leaves are a natural attractant to insects and fungus.
- Remove insect homes, pull weeds and weak or infected plants quickly. This lessens the likelihood of a few pests becoming a colony.
- Plant known detractors. If you are planting tomatoes and know that bug A really likes tomatoes but hates cucumbers, then plant cucumbers around the tomatoes. This is a great natural defense.

Animal Farming

Animal farming can also be a great staple to aid your off grid diet and it may also have some welcome byproducts.

What Animals To Get

Consider raising chickens for meat, but also take into account that instead of just meat you also get eggs. Cows for meat can produce milk, as well as goats and goats can be kept in any decent sized garden. Sheep can be raised for mutton and for wool for clothing.

One of the best parts about animal farming is that after you cover the initial expense, if you plan right (i.e. get males and females), you may not need to purchase animals again.

Educate Yourself

Of course there is a bit to learn in order to pull off farming animals properly. How much do you know about taking care of animals? What will you do if your animal becomes sick or injured and there's no vet around? So you've raised a cow, how do you slaughter and butcher it? How do you make hamburger meat? Steak? The answers to these vary from animal to animal and there is a lot to learn.

If you are serious about keeping livestock you will need to thoroughly educate yourself. In preparation perhaps you could even volunteer to work with your local butcher, or a local farmer for free to see what you can learn from them.

Feeding Your Livestock

Something that people often forget is that meat is incredibly wasteful. You will have to feed your livestock precious food that could sustain you for a long time in order to get back a comparatively tiny amount of meat. This problem can be countered to some extent by keeping grazing animals such as cows, but that is of course only if you have a very large field at your disposal.

I would suggest keeping just chickens for eggs, if you can keep them fed properly that is. If you don't feed them well, then they won't be laying many eggs. Oats in the summer and whole corn in the winter are great ways to keep chickens laying. But these are also valuable foods that you can eat yourself. So keeping livestock, even basic livestock like chickens, will require an excess of foods so that you have enough to keep them fed. You can start preparing for this eventuality right now however by getting some corn and oats growing in your garden and only feeding your chickens feed that you have grown yourself. Once the chickens are fed, see how much you have left over.

One important note about farming that counts for both plants and animals is that "You are what you eat". This is very true and as you raise your crops and livestock you will have a large say in what chemicals and nutrients go into their systems. Because what they eat, you will eventually be eating as well. Perhaps a great aspect of living off grid is the need and desire to farm in a sustainable way, ensuring that your little slice of heaven is around for generations and that your family is a healthy as they can be.

Prepare for the Worst

Remember that you can't always expect your animals to live through every season or even to not get sick. Shortage of food and water and other factors may cause an untimely decline in your livestock. It is recommended that just like with vegetables and fruits you store away surplus meats for that inevitable rainy day.

Storage and Preservation

So you've successfully raised some crops and livestock now what? Most fruits and vegetables are not year round producers so you've got to have a way to preserve some of that food for winter.

You should be canning excess food and storing it so that you are well prepared for the long hard months of winter. But being prepared for winter is not your only concern. While you may take every precaution to have bountiful crops each year, you are not in control of the most important factor, the weather.

A late frost, a drought, an excessive amount of rainfall can all be detrimental to the success of your crops each year. In order to keep food on the table you should be planting and harvesting a surplus to put back each year. There are two major types of canning operations and are suitable for specific food varieties.

Water Bath Canning

For canning highly acidic foods (think tomatoes and fruits) water bath canning can be used. Water bath canning involves filling your jar with the desired produce, placing the lid and band on and then boiling the jar in hot water. This boiling process forces out all of the air in the jar and creates a sort of super seal to keep air and bacteria from getting in. The key to successful canning is in essence, stopping the aging process of the food.

For water bath canning, you will need a deep metal container that is deep enough to cover the lid of the jars inside. You also ideally want a rack to sit the cans on as sitting the jars on the bottom of the metal container can cause them to crack. You don't need a rack however, you could simply place a folded up cloth in the bottom to keep them off of the metal.

Of course you will need some jars and some good quality canning lids for those jars. Standard jars and lids aren't safe to use as the seal most likely won't be good enough.

High Pressure Canning

For mixing high acid and low acid foods, or for simply canning low acid foods the high pressure canning method is used. This allows you store meat and vegetables safely and provides a nice fresh taste when the jars are finally opened and used. Pressure canning heats the contents of the can to 240 degrees Fahrenheit (water bath only goes to 212 degrees Fahrenheit). Why do you need the extra 28 degrees? Botulism.

Botulism spores can still survive in low acid foods prepared under

240 degrees. High pressure canning allows you to safely ensure your food will be ready when you are ready to eat it. The main difference between the two types of canning other than temperature, is the addition of one more tool for pressure canning. This tool is the pressure canner; they can range from $80 to $300.

For pressure canning, you will again need jars and lids but this time instead of a deep metal container you will need a pressure cooker.

If you want to get good at canning, there's only one way to do it. Get a recipe book and get practicing! Grow and can everything you can. This way you will start to learn the process and also learning how much you will need to grow and store to sustain yourself and your family.

Preserving Meat

Meat has the advantage of being able to be slaughtered at any time of year, whereas fruit and veg is seasonal. Even so, you're probably not going to want to eat the whole animal in one go so you're going to need ways of preserving it.

The two main ways of preserving meat are smoking to make jerky and salting to cure the meat.

Smoking and Jerky

To smoke meat you will obviously need a fire to produce the smoke and heat needed to dry the meat. It's important to have a smoking rack and a fire set up so that you can put the meat that you are going to be smoking straight onto it as soon as it's butchered.

The smoking rack needs to be at least a few feet above the fire as you don't want to cook the meat. If the meat starts to cook it can start to become dangerous and may contain botulism.

After about 24-48 hours, depending on the temperature and wind levels etc. you will have some nice smoked jerky. You can add spices etc. during the smoking process if you want to add to the flavor. Also you don't have to smoke it, you could leave it to air dry, but it will taste really bland. You can also up the smokiness by wrapping your rack in a tarp or by laying some braches over it to keep the smoke in.

Salting and Curing

Salting is a very simple process and it has been recorded as a method of preserving meat in ancient history texts that pre-date even the Romans.

To get started, just set up an area where you can salt your meat, so a good sized work surface is ideal. Then rub salt into the meat very generously before letting it sit for 12-14 days. This meat will keep for a very long time and you can eat it as and when you like.

How to Preserve Eggs for Months

Believe it or not, but you can actually get eggs to last for at least 8 months! It's very simple too. All you need to do is submerge them in lime water. So get a jar and make a lime/water mixture. It doesn't have to be airtight as long as there is a lid so that the water doesn't evaporate they will be fine.

When testing this, 100% of the eggs lasted 8 months but they could potentially last even longer. Just make sure you use slaked lime, also called hydrated lime. This is different to lime used in gardening. As a general rule use about an Ounce of Lime for a 1 Quart container.

Renewable Energy

So you want to live off grid, but most of us don't want to completely give up the perks of electric power. Thankfully there are some alternative energy solutions available to us.

Solar Power

Solar power has become increasingly more affordable and complete solar panel kits are easy to find and relatively easy for the do it yourselfer to install on their own. With the right system it is feasible to power your entire home on solar power alone, and utilizing a battery back-up can eliminate the need to rely on a power company at night.

Solar panels are generally installed south facing in the norther hemisphere to obtain as much sunlight as possible during the day. Some systems use "net-metering" wherein if you live on a grid you "sell" power back to the electric company and receive money off your bill at an agreed rate. A net-metered system affords the homeowner the ability to turn off the grid supply during an outage and keep their power running in their home from solar use.

Solar power clearly has many advantages, though whole home kits are still a bit expensive and not nearly as efficient as they are predicted to become in the future.

To understand more about the costs of solar power you should first understand what your home requires to be fully powered. A great helper in this endeavor is PV Watts calculator online at PVWatts.nrel.gov

Remember the cardinal rule of creating your own power: you must use less than you create. So when you are estimating usage, estimate high (you'll thank yourself later) and be realistic about power consumption. In all seriousness, you should crunch the numbers and then crunch them again.

Mini Solar Panels

You can get small solar panels in a whole variety of shapes and sizes. If you just need enough electricity to run a radio or charge phones etc. then one of these small panels may be perfect for you.

They can also be used in bug out situations as they are easily portable. Some recommendations would be the Anker 14W and the ALLPOWERS 12W both of which are very affordable and compact.

Wind power

Another highly popular form of electricity generation involves utilizing the wind. If you've driven through the Midwest United States, or through German and French countryside you have probably seen the large white futuristic looking windmills.

Windmills let the wind do the work to fire an electromagnetic generator. In essence, the wind spins the blades, which spin a large winding of copper around a magnetic core. In return, this action creates electrical current which is then transported from the windmill to the power grid. While you don't need a monster sized windmill to power your home, you will need a bit more time, patience and some do it yourself skill to make it happen.

Again vital to understanding the size of wind turbine needed is understanding your power usage. There are vast troves of knowledge to be found on the internet to help you understand the numbers, and no, you don't have to be an electrician or have an engineering degree.

Home Security

So you've got a family, crops and livestock and you're sitting pretty. How do you protect what you have worked so hard for? Thinking about home security is something that should happen before an incident, not after. You don't want to spend a day Monday morning quarterbacking all the what-ifs after you've maybe lost an important part of your sustainability. No one ever expects their house to catch fire, but nearly everyone has a smoke detector and a fire extinguisher.

But having the tools is not enough. In off grid living, the likelihood that you will be able to get the police rushing to the scene of the crime within 60 seconds is slim, and depending on the case that's led you to live off grid, it could be none. So you need to be prepared for a variety of situations and everyone should have a good idea of their roles and responsibilities during these scenarios. The best security for your home is knowledge. Let's face it, you cannot possibly prepare for any and all scenarios that may occur, as mentioned previously. The best thing to do is make sure everyone knows what to do in case of an emergency. Depending on said emergency you will need to be comfortable with a variety of skills. There are definitely so many more that could make the list but here's a rough breakdown of what the most important skills and plans will be.

Basic First Aid

At least one person with an advanced knowledge of first aid is absolutely required. This can be the difference between life and death in even some commonplace scenarios, especially in an off grid world. Knowing how to identify and subsequently treat a simple allergic reaction, bee sting, snake bite, or poison ingestion will be critical in a world where medical care no longer a phone call away. Having everybody aware of the signs and symptoms as well as quick treatment options will make for a much better long term prognosis to off grid survival. An advanced first aid respondent will be able to deal with harder solutions, such as broken appendages and severe sicknesses.

Medical Supplies

You will of course need the relevant medical supplies to allow the first aider to do their job properly. The basic medical supplies that you should have in your home at all times are antiseptic fluid and a range of dressings and bandages. You should also keep backup supplies of painkillers and any other medications you may specifically require.

If you want to get more advanced with your medical supplies there are some great items that you can get to help with more serious injuries. The SWAT-T Tourniquet will enable you to reduce the blood flow to an extremity and help stop excessive bleeding. Also the Quikclot Sport 50 Gram can be used instead of a standard dressing and the enzyme it contains will cause wounds to clot and stop bleeding much faster. These both make fantastic additions to a first aid kit and will allow you to treat much more serious wounds and potentially save a life.

Communication Plans and Rendezvous Points

You cannot expect for real life situations to follow what you've practiced to a T. It's important for everyone to know how to keep in contact with each other and have designated meeting places and times should communications become disrupted. Everyone on the team needs to know this information by heart, and should communications checkups or rendezvous point times be missed, everyone needs to be aware of how to handle that situation as well.

What does that mean? Say you all split up in the woods while foraging for morel mushrooms, you've all designated to meet at appointed spot A after three and a half hours of mushroom hunting. Person C of the group does not show up, and for some reason the walkie-talkies aren't working, now what? Do you assume person C is okay to get back on their own? Do you go looking for person C? This is why having rough plans is better than having no plans.

Hand to Hand Combat Training (Self Defense)

So who knows what situation has led to your off-grid living, but if it's something dire as in the case of a total societal breakdown, then it's probably safe to assume that there are going to be bad people out there who are unable to help themselves, looking for people like you to help them, possibly under threat of violence.

Knowing how to defend yourselves in a close-quarters situation can be vital to your survival. Knowing some self-defense moves is not enough, you should be actively practicing to keep your skills honed and ready. As stated before, no one wants a house fire, but everyone has smoke detectors and fire extinguishers. It's a twofold benefit really, you are prepared for something you hope to never face, and you get the added benefit of fitness to help you in all your endeavors. Because there are no two attacks that are the same you should study a variety of different disciplines to provide for the best defense possible. 2 styles that are currently quite popular and cover a wide variety of scenarios are Wing Chun Kung Fu and the Israeli Krav Maga.

Weapons Training

Of course like a fire extinguisher, people own weapons in the hopes that they never need to use them. However needing to use one and not knowing how is just as deadly as needing one and not having one.

Knowing how to safely and effectively use your weapons can be the difference between success and failure, and when failure with weapons is involved you can count on it being catastrophic.

Like everything else mentioned previously you should practice and practice again. But it's not enough for you to know how to use these weapons; everyone on your team should be able to use them as well. Proper firearms (and all weapons) safety should be the first thing covered.

Secondly, you should focus on how to be proficient with your weapon. This means efficiently loading, firing, reloading and being able to do so accurately. But training with a single weapon is not enough, because there's no guarantee that your preferred weapon is going to be readily available. Training with everyday items is crucial, these include knives (both pocket and kitchen), bats, bars, clubs, sticks, rocks, slingshots, screwdrivers, basically anything you can get your hands on at a time of desperate need.

Retreating

Do you have a plan for if things go really bad? If you have to run and leave your homestead, does everyone on your team know the plan? Did you set rendezvous points? Do you have a communication plan? It's important to plan for this so that when all hell breaks loose it can be an almost automatic reaction.

Success in the Off Grid World

As you may have noticed so far there is a strong emphasis on preparation throughout this guide. What you may not have picked up on quite as much is the emphasis on teamwork. It is my belief that in order to survive off the grid, we will need to work together.

Community

In fact the basic needs of a group of humans to be together likely derive from the ability of a group to share a load and better provide for everyone. Having a group of family or friends that you can rely on is going to be pivotal to everyone's success in the off grid world.

In essence, you need your own mini community, where everyone has certain assignments and shares the load. This may sound a little like communism and maybe it is, but in essence off grid living could be a world where money no longer means anything and a full belly means everything.

Communal living allows for its residents to put their heads together to solve problems, lessen the workload for everyone and since everyone has a vested interest in the survival of the community, provide for security awareness and preparation.

Preparation

There's that word again, preparation. Why is it used so much? Why do I harp on it? Put simply there's no real way to be prepared for anything, but our bodies and minds are a bit more reflexive than we give them credit for. Knowing a weapon inside and out, and being able to efficiently use it can cause a sort of drone like reaction comes when the adrenaline pumps and everything happens insanely fast. Knowing who to communicate with and when is vital and can be reflexive as well. The same can be said for rendezvous points.

In short when we train to do something over and over again, it becomes a second nature to do that thing when it is needed the most. Off grid living (especially dependent on the circumstance) does not allow for many mistakes to be forgiven. You may simply have only your knowledge base to rely on when the chips are all down. So simply put, no, you can never be too prepared or rehearsed.

When sports players become legends they often do so because they have focused on one thing throughout their career, the basics. The Harlem Globetrotters weren't born with some amazing ball dribbling talent, they practiced it, and practiced it and practiced it, and then they practiced it some more. Even now that they are really good at doing ball tricks they are still practicing them, every day.

The same goes for preparing, you must practice. Once again, you cannot rehearse every situation that the world will throw at you, but you can have rudimentary plans in place that give yourself and everyone on your team an idea of how to handle situations as they come up. Life itself is full of challenges and off grid life is no exception to this. Having a handle on how to respond can make the road a little less challenging and life a little more comfortable.

Practice

Keep in mind that many of the items mentioned in this beginners guide are just the tip of the iceberg, a broad paint stroke in an otherwise much more specific painting. Gardening overviews are great, but to become a true green thumb you need to practice. Hunting sounds particularly easy in print, however make sure you practice so that you become better at bringing home game and less prone to falling asleep in the woods (trust me, it happens).

Irrigation also sounds easy when you read a synopsis of what it means, but digging a well isn't as easy as buying the right tool and starting to dig. Keep in mind that as humans we have evolved over time to become better at certain things, but sometimes this means we have lost other talents we once had.

Preparation and planning are the two greatest assets to a successful transition and because the world we live in can be so unpredictable you can't assume that every year's harvest will yield the same results. If you have a surplus of crops, can it and store it for the year when hardships abound.

Having a knowledgeable team with certain dedicated roles can make the workload less and life more fruitful, but simply having one person trained and in one role is not a good failsafe. Try cross training, everyone has their specific skill set, however they should be trained and practiced in a different skill set as a backup.

All members of the team should be well versed in basic first aid, weapons and defense skills, farming and hunting. But they should be also trained in a specificity such as butchering, or advanced first aid, or advanced defense tactics, electricity generation and electrical systems repair.

These are just a few things to think about with regards to training your team. And remember, to just be trained in something is not enough; to experience true proficiency is to practice and practice and practice again. Here are a few more considerations before moving to a completely off grid life style.

Money

Erase your debt, completely. Preparing to live off grid can be expensive, especially if you are starting almost totally from scratch. Make sure you have no debts going in to your new life, and since we're on the subject of money…stockpile some cash for a seriously rainy day.

Off grid living doesn't require much in the way of income when you become completely self-sustaining, however it's good to sock away some cash in case things get really, really dark. What if you have several catastrophic events that affect your food supply, power supply and overall quality of life? Having a little nest egg stored up can be the difference between scraping together meals and still living comfortably while you right the ship.

Trade your skills for others' or for services. Generally speaking you can probably barter with other likeminded folks to get some staples you might be missing or haven't figured out. Sustainable living doesn't have to be uncomfortable living and it definitely doesn't mean you can't work if you want to. If you've got a valued trade or skill you can certainly reap the rewards from this.

Location

Learn about the indigenous life around your new home. It is good to know about natural threats and predators, but also you should know what sort of nutrients your surroundings have to offer. Can you forage for edible nuts and berries? Are there edible mushrooms in the area? More importantly, are there berries and mushrooms in the area that you should steer clear of? Where does most of the game bed down? Are there streams for fishing? Wood for chopping?

These things might seem a bit trivial but you should really know the lay of the land, and seek to learn more about it with each passing day. After all you are going to have an ongoing give and take, love and hate relationship with this land. You should know it better than anyone. You will be its steward and it will be yours.

Thanks For Reading!

I sincerely hope you enjoyed this book and gained some useful information along the way.

If you want to stay up to date with my regular free book promotions and to also find out about my future releases you can sign up to my mailing list at - www.southshorepublications.com/steverayder

If you would also consider taking the time to leave me an honest review on this book on Amazon I would be extremely appreciative of your feedback.

You can find links to all of my previous books on my author profile at http://www.amazon.com/Steve-Rayder/e/B00U0U3Z3E/ or by searching for "Steve Rayder" on Amazon.

Thanks for reading and I hopefully speak to you all in the next book!

www.ingramcontent.com/pod-product-compliance
Lightning Source LLC
Chambersburg PA
CBHW070826290526
45795CB00002B/845